SUPERSTUDIES
for violin

Really easy original studies for the young player

Ganz einfache Originaletüden für Angfänger

Études originales et très faciles pour les jeunes musiciens

Mary Cohen

© 1993 by Faber Music Ltd

First published in 1993 by Faber Music Ltd

3 Queen Square London WC1N 3AU

Printed in England

ISBN 0-571-51421-9

FABER ff MUSIC

Symbol	Name	Beats
𝅝	semibreve	4
𝅗𝅥	minim	2
𝅘𝅥	crotchet	1
𝅘𝅥𝅮	quaver	$\frac{1}{2}$
𝅘𝅥𝅯	semiquaver	$\frac{1}{4}$

⊓ down - pull

V up - push

Slurs ⌣
Share the bow
Stroke equally
between the 2
notes.

To buy Faber Music publications or to find out about the full range of titles available
please contact your local music retailer or Faber Music sales enquiries:

Faber Music Limited, Burnt Mill, Elizabeth Way, Harlow, CM20 2HX England
Tel: +44 (0)1279 82 89 82   Fax: +44 (0)1279 82 89 83
sales@fabermusic.com   www.fabermusic.com

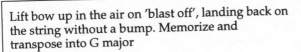

1. Blast Off!

Lift bow up in the air on 'blast off', landing back on the string without a bump. Memorize and transpose into G major	Beim 'blast off' den Bogen abheben und dann wieder auf den Saiten landen lassen, ohne zurückzufedern. Auswendig lernen und nach G-Dur transponieren.

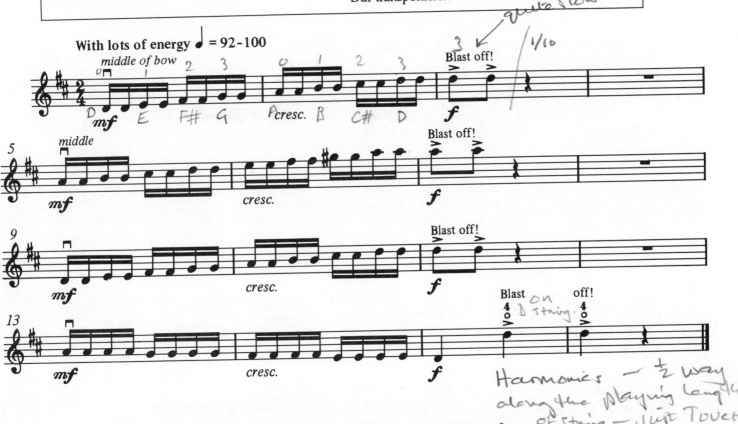

2. Operation Space Station

1- and 2-octave harmonics	1- und 2-oktavige Flageoletti

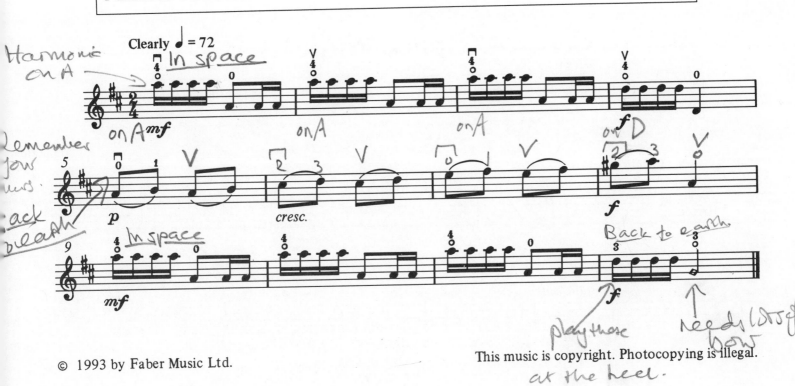

3. Rockets to the Rescue

Relaxed bow-hold and balanced arm movement in semiquavers. Scale passages

Entspannte Bogenhaltung und ausbalancierte Armbewegung bei den Sechzehnteln. Tonleiterpassagen

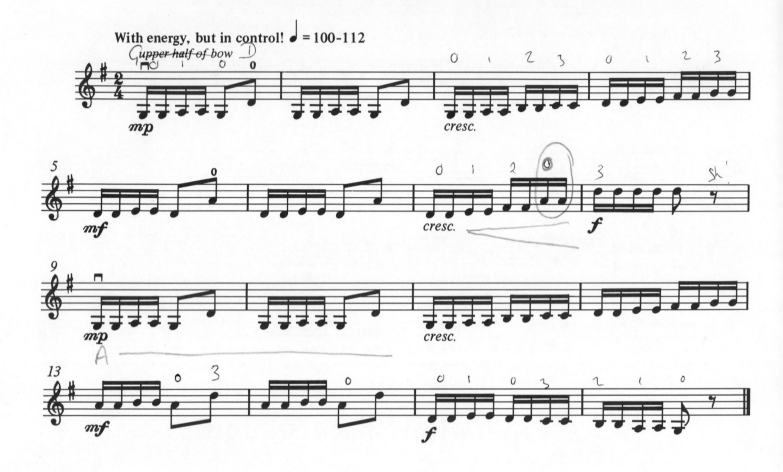

4. Space Walk

Stay anchored to your base – don't let the first finger drift!

Auf der Basisstation bleiben – nicht mit dem ersten Finger vom Kurs abweichen!

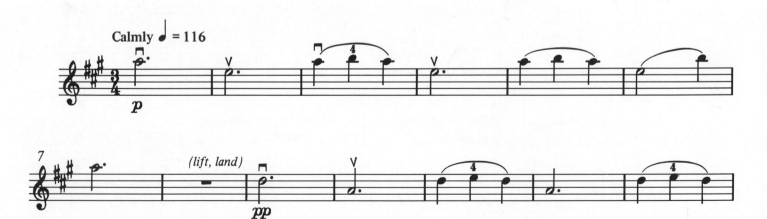

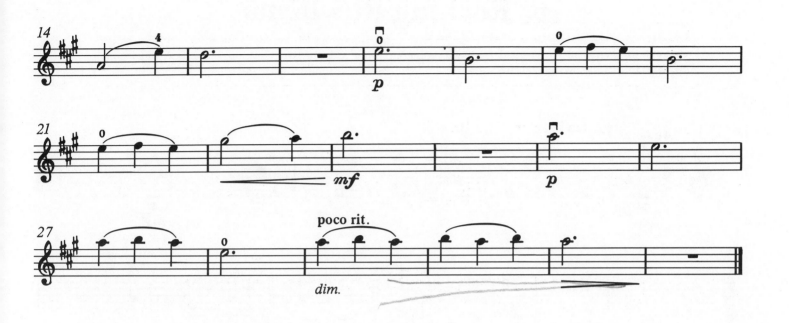

5. Robots Rocking at the Microchip Ball

Use all of your right arm to help you reach the strings. Occasionally try this piece still pizzicato, but with the bow in your hand

Den ganzen rechten Arm dazu benutzen, die Saiten zu erreichen. Gelegentlich das Stück auch im *pizzicato* spielen, aber mit dem Bogen in der Hand

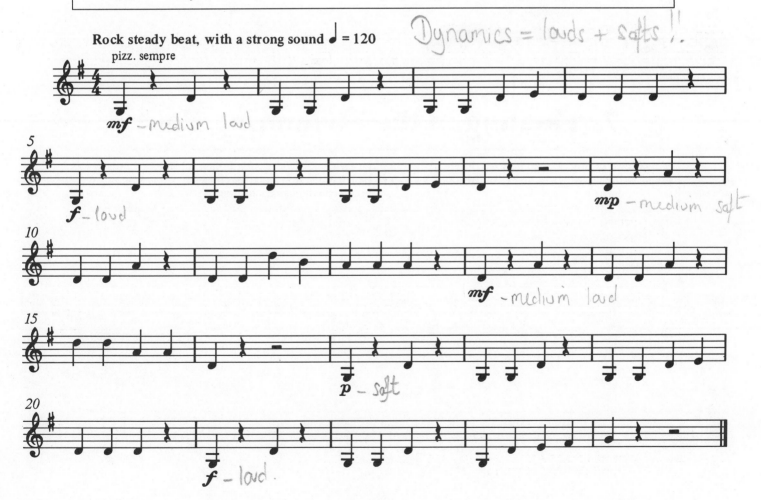

4

6. Rocking Rowboats

Smooth string-crossing; slurs; good arm position for tone and intonation on the G string

Weiter Saitenwechsel; Bindungen; gute Armhaltung für den Ton und die Intonation auf der G-Saite

7. Floating in the Swimming Pool

Slow bows, saving enough bow for the ends of notes; string crossings in different directions

Langsame Striche; genug Bogen für das Ende der Noten aufsparen Saitenwechsel in unterschiedlichen Richtungen

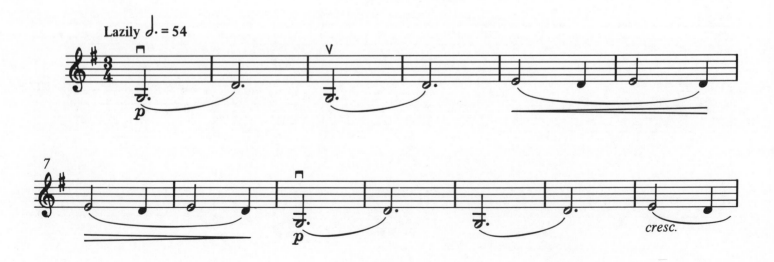

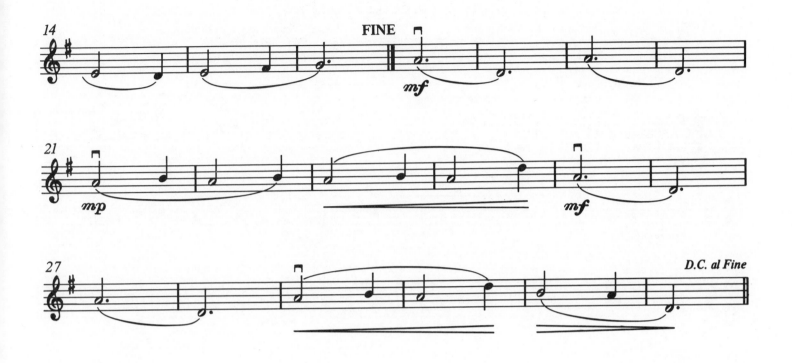

8. Wave Machine

Let your right arm bob along with the waves   Den rechten Arm mit den Wellen schwingen lassen

6

9. Gliding along at the Octopus Ball

Smooth bowing; finding octave harmonics;
checking tuning of octaves

Weiche Striche; Oktavflageoletti finden; die
Stimmung der Oktaven prüfen

10. Hear that Whistle!

Linked bows; glissandos and harmonics for the
train whistles; good 3rd finger tuning in 1st position

Dichte Striche; *glissandi* und Flageoletti für die
Eisenbahnpfeifen; gute Intonation des 3. Fingers in
der 1. Lage

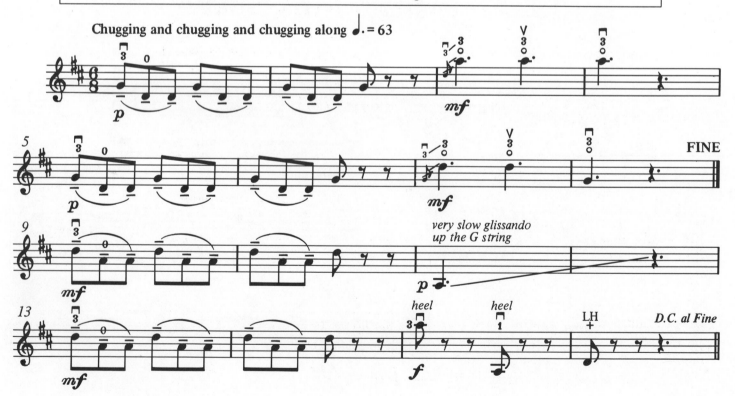

11. Hurry if you want to see the Engine!

Simple, slow trills; keeping a relaxed bow-hold in the semiquavers; contrasting dynamics (Can you work out the story this piece tells?)

Einfache, langsame Triller; bei den Sechzehnteln eine entspannte Bogenhaltung beibehalten; gegensätzliche Dynamiken. (Kannst Du Dir denken, worum es in dieser Geschichte geht?)

12. Strawberry Milk Shake

[1 = place 1st finger across both strings
1_____ hold finger down on string
Watch out in bar 12!

[1 = den 1. Finger über beide Saiten halten
1_____ den Finger unten auf der Saite halten
Vorsicht in Takt 12

8

13. Toffee Nut Fudge Cake

Neat bowing; nimble fingering; introducing 'sliding semitones'

Saubere Striche; wendige Fingersätze; Einführung von 'gleitenden Halbtönen'

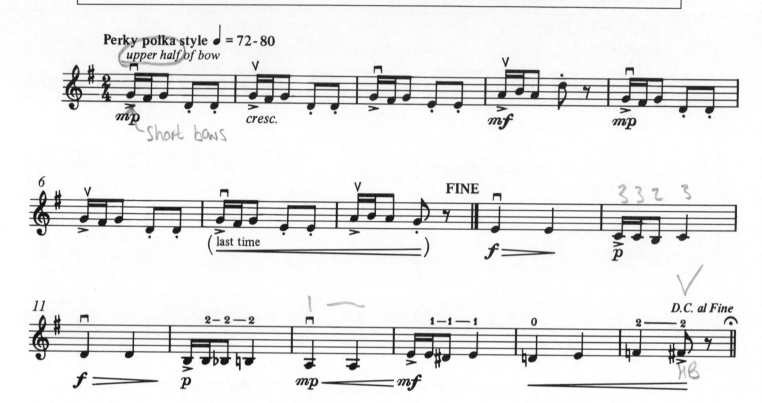

14. Rum-Bah Ba!

Practise ♩. ♩. ♪ 𝄽 on 1 note until you can
Rum-Bah Ba
really *feel* the rhythm
Watch out in bars 8 and 16

♩. ♩. ♪ 𝄽 auf einem Ton üben, bis man
Rum - Bah Ba
den Rhythmus wirklich *fühlt*.
Vorsicht in den Takten 8 und 16

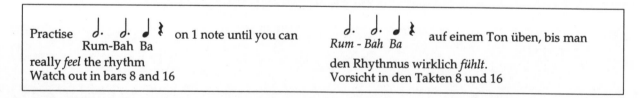

15. Vanilla Ice Cream

Practise ♩ | ♪♩ ♪♪ Va - nil-la ice cream with the correct bowing on 1 note several times to get the feel of the rhythm	♩ | ♪♩ ♪♪ Va - nil-la ice cream mit richtiger Bogenführung auf einem Ton mehrere Male üben, um das Rhythmusgefühl zu trainieren

16. Cuckoo? Where's that Cuckoo?

Keep the 2nd finger close to the string at all times to act as a guide for the 3rd finger; contrasting echo dynamics; simple octave harmonics

Den 2. Finger dicht an der Saite halten, um dem 3. Finger die Orientierung zu erleichtern; gegensätzliche Echodynamik; einfache Oktavflageoletti

17. Let's all go to the Grizzly Bear's Grump

Dotted rhythms in linked bows; good tone on lower strings

Punktierte Rhythmen bei dichten Strichen; guter Ton auf den tiefen Saiten

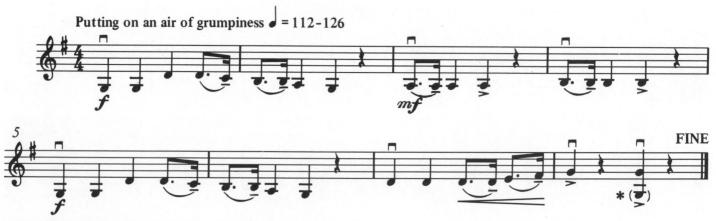

* last time add lower octave

18. Tawny Owl Blues

Practise saying the words first; crisp rhythmic
bowing; very steady beat throughout

Zuerst einmal üben, die Wörter zu sprechen;
rhythmisch prägnante Striche; immer fest im
Metrum bleiben

✱ optional tremolo on last note

19. Banana Bounce

Bounce the bow on the spot, then add tiny sideways 'bananas', spiccato! Notice how the bow bounces best nearest the heel on the G string when you are playing *f* and nearer the middle on the E string in *p*

Den Bogen auf der Stelle springen lassen und dann etwas seitlicher *'Bananas' spiccato* spielen. Der Bogen springt im *f* auf der G-Saite am Frosch und im *p* auf der E-Saite in der Bogenmitte am besten.

'Ba - na - nas!'

'Ba - na - nas?'   'Oh   yeah!'

VIOLIN MUSIC FOR THE BEGINNER FROM FABER MUSIC

Mary Cohen's Superseries

Mary Cohen's *Superseries* has been hailed by string teachers worldwide as a breakthrough in violin teaching. Springing from Mary's unique pupil-centred approach to technical and musical learning, it encourages self-motivation and musicianship from the very first lesson.

The series covers work for the absolute beginner up to the advanced player.

'Be grateful to Cohen for her insight, imagination,
and the application of her ideas in teaching different violin skills.'
(*Music Teacher*)

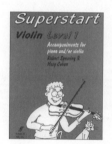

Superstart

*Basic skills and pieces
for beginners*

LEVEL 1 ISBN 0-571-51319-0 (violin part)
LEVEL 1 ISBN 0-571-51711-0 (piano acc.)
LEVEL 2 ISBN 0-571-51705-6 (violin part)
LEVEL 2 ISBN 0-571-51712-9 (piano acc.)

Superpieces

*Additional repertoire
for violin and piano*

BOOK 1 ISBN 0-571-51869-9 (complete)
BOOK 1 ISBN 0-571-51871-0 (violin part)
BOOK 2 ISBN 0-571-51870-2 (complete)
BOOK 2 ISBN 0-571-51872-9 (violin part)

Superstudies

*Original studies for the
young player*

BOOK 1 ISBN 0-571-51421-9
BOOK 2 ISBN 0-571-51450-2

Superduets

*Original and entertaining
duets for beginner violinists*

BOOK 1 ISBN 0-571-51889-3
BOOK 2 ISBN 0-571-51890-7

Scaley Monsters

*Scales without tears for
young violinists*

ISBN 0-571-51423-5

Space it!

*Easy well-known pieces
for violin*

ISBN 0-571-51806-0

FABER ff MUSIC